This book belongs to:

_____

THE BEST
COUNTING BOOK
IN THE
WILD WEST

TEXT BY MADELINE BENNETT
ILLUSTRATIONS BY GARY BENNETT

Featuring Accounting Cricket

And the Buffalo Bug Band

Two numbers are hidden in each big picture. Follow Accounting Cricket's hints to find one of them. If you're stumped on the other, check out the special clues on the last page.

Bubba

Buster

Billy-Bob

and Paul

The illustrations were created with Adobe Illustrator.
The text was set in Goudy Book, bold, and extra bold.
Cover display text was set in Futura.

Designed by Gary Bennett
Edited by Bob Early

Prepared by the Book Division of *Arizona Highways*© magazine, a monthly
publication of the Arizona Department of Transportation.

Publisher — Nina M. La France
Managing Editor — Bob Albano
Associate Editor — Evelyn Howell
Art Director — Mary Winkelman Velgos
Production Director — Cindy Mackey

Printed in Hong Kong.
Library of Congress Catalog Card Number: 00-103253
ISBN 1-893860-13-2

ARIZONA HIGHWAYS
BOOKS

To mom and dad,
my sister and brothers:
For roller-skating, hide and seek,
church camp on the lake. For pillow fights,
ocean swims, the wind-up doll, too. For
drive-in movies and tucking me in,
and all that you still do.
– Love, "Squirt"

To Aunt Gloria and the Wentworths:
For herding sheep, pickle farming, motor bikes,
UFOs, fallout shelters, corncob pipes,
rotten egg fights and trips to the outhouse
on cold winter nights.
– G.B.

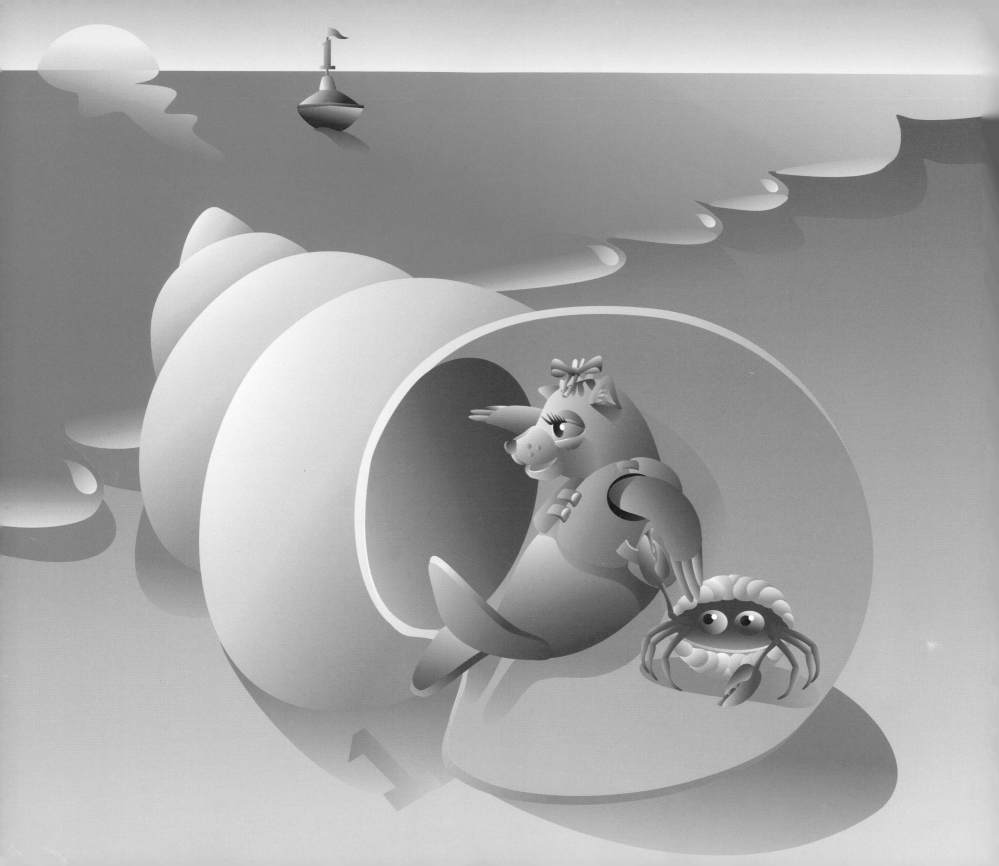

1

Sadie Seal is so very small,
She can count to 1 and that's all.

But Sadie can share easily.
That's 1 for you and 1 for me.
Sadie has 1 special shell,
She takes care of very well.

She also has 1 special pal,
A little crab she knows as Sal.
They sit at the seashore all day long,
And share the sound of the seashell song.

Sadie knows you can't go wrong,
If you have 1 friend, 1 shell, 1 special song.

For the hidden
number 1 look:
1. On the sand.
2. In Sadie's hand.
3. In starfish land.

2

Bunion Big Foot likes hide-n-seek.
He's so patient he can hide for a week.

The giant redwoods are his playground.
He can hide in the trees and just fool around.

He can blend his legs into the trees.
But his 2 feet stick out below his knees.

He can hide 2 arms; they won't be a surprise.
He can hide his head with his 2 brown eyes.

He can hide 2 ears, that's easy to do.
But, he can't hide his 2 big feet, 1-2.

If you were looking for
the hidden 2 would you:
1. Go to a dude ranch?
2. Look at a tree branch?
3. Ask Aunt Blanche?

3

Little Barkley Beaver, only 3 years old,
Brushes his 3 teeth without being told.

Barkley, who cuts twigs and bark
The whole day long,
Needs to brush his 3 teeth
To keep them clean and strong.

If you don't brush your teeth
To keep them cavity-free
You won't be able to eat at all
If your diet is a tree.

The number 3
is hidden somewhere.
Would you find it:
1. On Barkley's face?
2. On Barkley's waist?
3. On Barkley's toothpaste?

The flag is flying high, the band is playing loud.
Remembering our 4-fathers makes us feel proud.

The 4-Hops look handsome in their 4 bow ties
As they join together to harmonize.

The 4-Fresh Mites sing their 4 favorite songs
As they invite the crowd to sing along.

The Buffalo Bug Band, Bubba, Buster, Billy-Bob, and Paul,
Reunite to play together, 4 hats and all.

To watch colorful fireworks light up the sky,
We'll stay up late on the 4th of July.

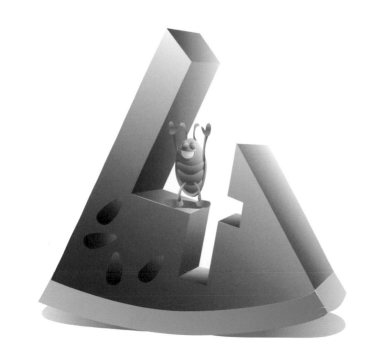

If Accounting Cricket wants
you to find the number **4**
you should look:
1. On the watermelon.
2. On his girlfriend, Helen.
3. He's not tellin'.

5

Herbie the Gila Monster turns 5 today.
And he celebrates in a very special way.

He invites 5 best friends who are already 5 years old.
They all bring him a present without being told.

Herbie's waited for this day all year long.
5 little voices sing the Happy Birthday song.

He blows out 5 candles on his birthday cake.
His 5 friends cheer, even Sidney the snake.

Now Herbie is 5, and knows he's a big shot.
"Just look at my tail," he says, "and my new 5th spot."

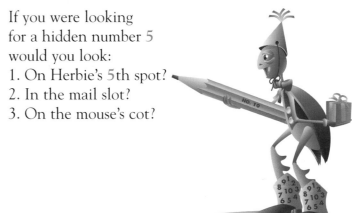

If you were looking
for a hidden number 5
would you look:
1. On Herbie's 5th spot?
2. In the mail slot?
3. On the mouse's cot?

6

The 6 quail sisters are all really cool.
Because the 6 quail sisters follow this simple rule:
Always do your homework, and never miss school.

Mary is good at history, Machelle reads very well.
Melanie likes art, Madeline can really spell.
Marta's best in sports, and Marilyn's no dumbbell.

These sisters 6 are all top-notch,
And that's the end of this tale.
'Cause as you know with no top-notch,
A quail is not a quail.

If you were looking for the hidden
number 6 would you look:
1. On a vine?
2. In a gold mine?
3. On a sign?

7

Now here's something you don't see everyday,
7 little prairie dogs floating away.
Their parents told them they could go out and play,
But not to blow bubbles on a windy day!

"Stay out of trouble, be home by dark,
"And come back on the double if you hear us bark."

They blew 7 bubbles anyway,
Ignoring what their parents had to say.
And as they started to float up in the sky,
All 7 little prairie dogs began to cry.

Then suddenly the wind stopped,
And they tumbled to the ground.
All 7 little prairie dogs, safe and sound.

So always listen to what your parents say,
Or you might float away
On the next windy day.

If you were looking for
the hidden number 7
you could look:
1. At a banana.
2. On the bandanna.
3. In Havana.

8 chipmunks chattering in the Chiricahuas.
Do you find that hard to say?
Try to listen to all 8 of them,
As they chitchat away.

All 8 friends getting up at 8.
All 8 voices heard from early 'til late,
Claudia, Christine, Carol and Charlene,
Connie, Carolyn, Colby and Angie Jean.

8 friends doing what they like to do.
8 friends with their own points of view.
8 friends who love to talk all day.
And all 8 can tell you what the others had to say.

If you want to find
the number 8 look:
1. On Angie's socks.
2. On the rocks.
3. At Goldilocks.

Kartchner Cavern's
DiamondBats

9

If Kartchner had **9** players on a baseball team
They might look like this in your wildlife dream:

9 bats hanging from stalactites in a row.
9 gloves, **9** hats, **9** baseball bats all ready to go.

Bud, the batboy, would awake the team at **9**.
To play **9** innings under moonlight is a really good time!

You'd know they were the DiamondBats,
When they showed up to play.
Since all **9** little bats always swing away.

THE
WORLD FAMOUS
"ACROBATS"
PERFORM A 9
AT 9 NIGHTLY.

If the number **9** were hidden
in Kartchner Caverns it
might be found:
1. On the stalactites.
2. On the stalagmites.
3. On Bud's tights.

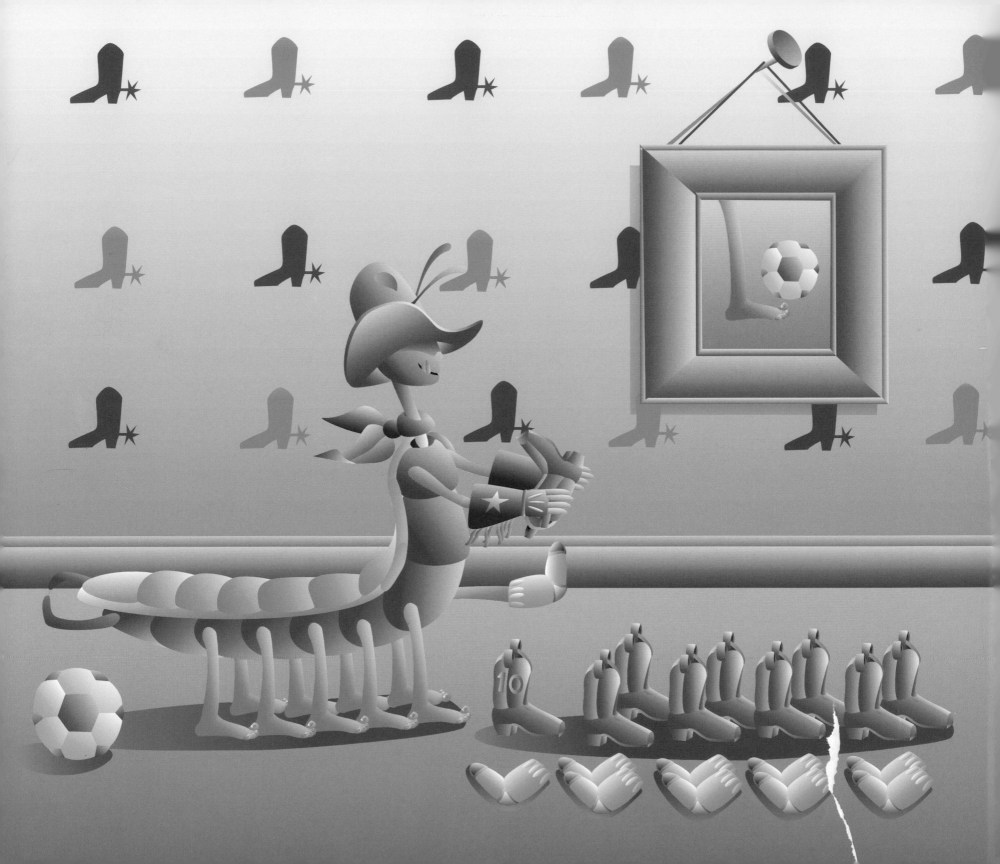

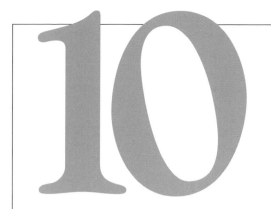

Now here's 10-a-pede Nick who's really neat.
Did I mention that he has 10 feet?
10 feet to tickle, 10 feet to itch,
So many toes to wiggle, so many toes to twitch.

Nick puts his 10 socks and 10 boots in a row.
So it takes little time to be ready to go.

10 feet can be trouble if you're in a hurry to play.
Putting 10 socks on 10 feet could take all day.

But Nick's a 10-a-pede who's organized.
If neatness were a contest he'd win first prize.

So when "Hurry up" is heard, "Let's go out and play."
He puts on 10 boots without wasting the day.

Where would you look
for the number 10:
1. On Nick's boot?
2. On Nick's snoot?
3. Isn't Nick cute?

It's easy to see the desert is a great place to be a bee.

You can pack a lunch or skateboard or just sightsee.

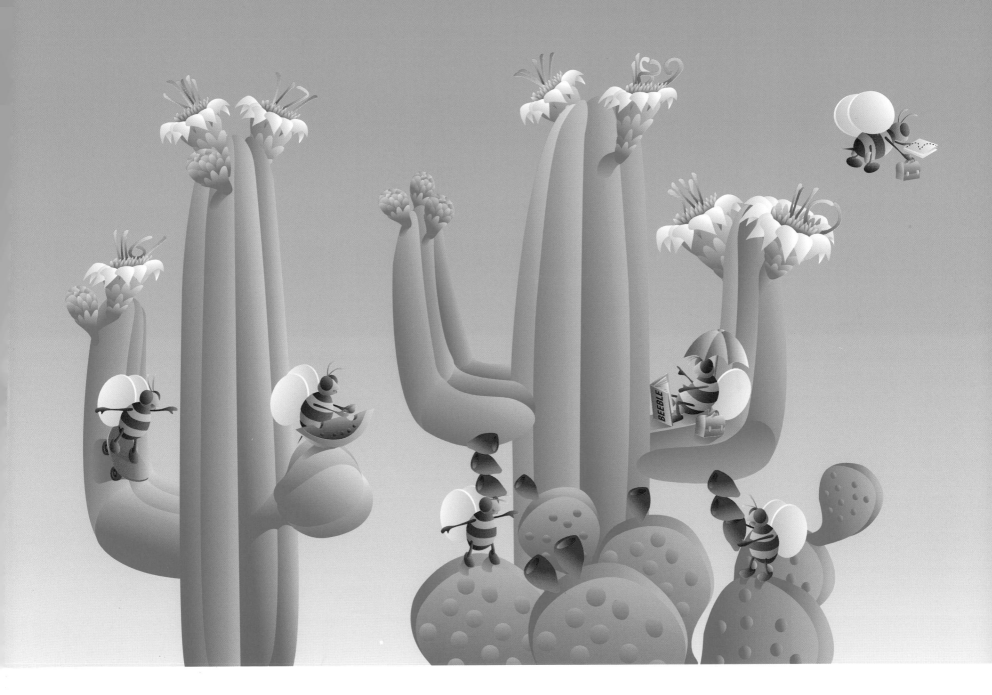

You can read a good book, or be busy as a bee and pick cactus fruit, all for free.
 Or you could find the numbers from 1 to 10. Let Accounting Cricket show you where to begin.

Little eaglets like their Rocky Mountains high.

They wear goggles, hats, and glasses as they learn how to fly.

Accounting Cricket points out the number 1. Start from there and have some fun.
Find each number from 1 to 10, then turn the page and count again.

There's a lot to see at the sea, like dolphins and whales and fish with sails.
And if you want to count 1 to 10, the starfish is where you might begin.

Or if you prefer, you can count each sea horse, or count each colored fish, of course.
Accounting Cricket will show you the 1 bubble. You'll find 2 to 10 without any trouble.

GLOSSARY

BAT: The only mammal that can fly. Bats are shy and live in caves or other dark, sheltered places. They hang upside down and only come out at night to eat. Some are as small as a bee and some are as large as a big bird.

BEAVER: A furry animal with a wide flat tail that looks like a paddle. They are good builders and can cut down trees with their sharp front teeth. They build log homes and dams. They are very good swimmers and can hold their breath under water for a long time.

BIG FOOT: A hairy humanlike creature said to live in the Pacific Northwest. Big Foot gets his name because people have reported seeing its huge footprints. It may or may not be real.

CENTIPEDE: An animal that looks like a worm or caterpillar. Its body is divided into segments, each with its own pair of legs. Its name means one hundred feet.

CHIPMUNK: A small brown animal that looks like a mouse with black and white stripes down the center of its back. It eats nuts and seeds and carries its food in its cheek pouches. It lives and sleeps through the winter in underground burrows, but likes to climb trees.

CHIRICAHUA (pronounced "cheer-ih-caw´-wah") **MOUNTAINS:** A mountain range in the Coronado National Forest in southeastern Arizona. It was named for the Chiricahua Apaches. Its name means "a great mountain."

EAGLET: A baby eagle. Born with its eyes open, it lives in a nest made of sticks and twigs high on a cliff or in a tree. Both parents take care of it. It learns to fly before it is a year old.

4TH OF JULY: The birthday of the United States of America. The day was chosen because the U.S. Congress adopted the Declaration of Independence on July 4, 1776.

GILA (pronounced "hee´-la") **MONSTER:** A desert lizard that looks like it's covered with orange and black beads. It grows to be almost two feet long, and is the only poisonous lizard in the U.S.

HONEY BEE: There are three kinds of bees in a colony. There are thousands of workers, a few hundred drones, and one queen bee. They make honey and beeswax.

KARTCHNER CAVERNS: A cave in southeastern Arizona. One of Arizona's state parks, it is filled with a lot of pointed rocks that look like large icicles growing from the ceiling and floor. It is called a "living" cave because these rocks, called stalagmites and stalactites, grow longer every year.

OCOTILLO (pronounced "ah-kuh-tee´-yo"): A desert plant with long, skinny branches that reach toward the sky. The branches are covered with sharp thorns. When it blooms in the spring, each branch gets a red blossom shaped like a flame on a candle.

OCELOT: A medium-size wildcat that has spots on its coat. It lives mainly in the forests of the Southwest. It hunts at night and sleeps in trees during the day.

PACIFIC OCEAN: A huge body of saltwater that covers more than one-third of the Earth's surface and is more than six miles deep in some places. It is home to all kinds of fish, plants, and animals.

GLOSSARY

PORPOISE: A sea mammal closely related to dolphins, but smaller. They can swim very fast. Some species are endangered.

PRAIRIE DOG: A rodent with short legs, light brown fur, and a short flat tail. It lives in large groups called towns. It gets its name because it makes a sound like a dog's bark.

PRICKLY PEAR CACTUS: A cactus made of a lot of rounded pads joined together. It is usually covered with sharp spines. Once a year it grows flowers which turn into red pear-shaped fruit. The fruit is so sweet that people make candy and jelly from it.

QUAIL: A small plump desert bird that makes its nest in the ground or on a low branch of a tree. A curly little feather sits on the top of its head. It can fly, but it usually runs along the ground.

RATTLESNAKE: A snake with a rattle on the end of its tail. The snake can hurt you if it bites you. Rattlesnakes cannot hear and are poisonous, so they should not be touched or picked up.

REDWOOD FOREST: Home of the evergreen trees that are the tallest in the world. They are found from Northern California to Oregon. Some are big enough to drive a car through.

ROCKY MOUNTAINS: The largest group of mountains in North America. They are 3,000 miles long and go through eight Western states.

SAGUARO (prounced "suh-wah´-ro") **CACTUS:** This cactus grows taller than other cacti and may live 200 to 300 years. As it gets older, it gets buds that grow to look like arms raised to the sky. It can live in the dry desert because it stores a lot of water inside its stem. Its white blossom is the official state flower of Arizona.

SCHOOL OF FISH: A group of fish that live together. There may be three fish or millions of fish in a school. Baby fish and adult fish are in different schools.

SEA HORSE: A tiny fish whose head looks like a horse. Baby sea horses form small groups by holding each other with their tails.

SEAL: A mammal with flippers instead of legs. It lives on land and in the sea. Some seals walk on their flippers and some seals move by hunching their bodies like a caterpillar.

STALACTITE: An icicle-shaped stone that grows from the ceiling inside a cave. It is made when water drips from the ceiling of a cave and dries. The minerals left behind grow together to look like long icicles. They come in many colors and get very big. Remember that stalactites grow from the ceiling, so it has a letter "c" in the middle.

STALAGMITE: A stone that looks like an upside-down icicle, which grows on the floor of caves. It is made when water drips from a stalactite and dries. The minerals left behind grow together and get very hard. Sometimes the stalagmite and the stalactite grow together and make one long piece from the ceiling to the ground. Remember that stalagmites grow from the ground, so it has a letter "g" in the middle.

STARFISH: A spiny-skinned sea animal that has no brain. It usually has five arms, and if one drops off it can grow another one. It has an eyespot on the tip of each arm and a mouth in the middle of its body.

**Clues to Find the Second Set
of Secret Numbers**

1 On the buoy.

2 On Big Foot's foot.

3 On the back stump.

4 In the fireworks.

5 On the middle candle.

6 On the apple.

7 In the grass.

8 On more rocks.

9 On a wooden bat.

10 The leg and ball
in the hanging picture.